Goldstein's Coca-Cola™ Collectibles

An Illustrated Value Guide

COLLECTOR BOOKS

A Division of Schroeder Publishing Co., Inc.

7536105

The current values in this book should be used only as a guide. They are not intended to set prices, which vary from one section of the country to another. Auctions prices as well as dealer prices vary greatly and are affected by condition as well as demand. The publisher does not assume responsibility for any losses that might be incurred as a result of consulting this guide.

Coca-Cola™ and Coke™ are registered trademarks which identify the same product of The Coca-Cola Company. Many of the items pictured herein are copyrighted in the name of The Coca-Cola Company.

If you have any questions regarding Coca-Cola™ collectibles, you may contact our advisor:
Gael de Courtivron
Buy - Sell - Trade - Appraisals
(941) 359-COLA (2652)

Additional copies of this book may be ordered from:

COLLECTOR BOOKS
P.O. Box 3009
Paducah, Kentucky 42002–3009

@$16.95. Add $2.00 for postage and handling
Copyright: Schroeder Publishing Co., Inc. 1991.
Updated Values, 1996

Printed by IMAGE GRAPHICS, INC., Paducah, Kentucky

Contents

Introduction

In 1971, Sheldon and Helen Goldstein released the first of four magnificent volumes on Coca-Cola™ advertising memorabilia. Mr. Goldstein had amassed a most remarkable collection and wanted to share his knowledge and pictures of his collection with the collecting public. These volumes published from 1971 through 1975 are now out of print. In 1990, Schroeder Publishing Co., Inc. purchased the film and copyrights to the four Goldstein books. We have combined most of the material taken from these books into this one presentation. Updated values have been included to reflect today's market prices.

As mentioned before, the four Goldstein books are now out of print and in time, will themselves become collector's items bringing premium prices.

Mr. Goldstein included a grading guide in Volume I that is noteworthy and repeated here. This guide pertains mostly to trays although he mentions that it can be used for "all Coca-Cola™ items that are collectible."

A Guide to Grading

We are using the same grading system that Mr. Goldstein used in the four volumes from which the material in this book was taken. He states that the grading system used for trays is "just as effective when grading paper, cardboard, glass, leather, and other materials used in the manufacture of Coca-Cola™ advertising memorabilia."

Mr. Goldstein further states that a special rare class has been established to separate the items made from 1898 thru 1904 because of their age and the limited number available to collectors today. He goes on to say that, "The grading system that we propose is one that will suffice for the early antique trays and items advertising Coca-Cola™ and all the other trays and items advertising Coke™ that are collectible."

Special Rare Class

Items falling in this class are the rare trays dating from 1898 through 1904. The values range from $1,500 to $10,000. These items need a special classification within themselves. For example: If there are two items, one, an 1898, and one, a 1940, both being in the same condition, the 1898, being the rarer of the two items, should be placed in a higher classification and the other item in a lower classification. When selling or trading an item in this special classification, one should photograph and describe in full detail any and all flaws in the item.

Special Reproduction Class

This classification should be included in the grading guide, because it falls in the category of collectibles advertising Coke™. They are also considered by many collectors and dealers as worthwhile trays and items to collect. These would be trays and items that are questionable, because they are unproven as to their authenticity. This class would also include trays and items proven to be reproduced and come in quantity. They should always be in mint condition because of their young age.

Mint Condition

New condition. In original unused condition. No visible marks.

Near Mint Condition

A classification in which most items that are thought of as mint would fall. Not in original mint condition. Upon inspection would show very minor or slight marks of age or usage.

Excellent Condition

Only minor scratch or scratches, hair-line type, visible on close examination. Small chip, chips or marks on outer rim or edge of tray or item.

Very Good Condition

Minor surface scratch or scratches. If any rust, not more than pinhead size. Minor flaking. Picture, lettering and color in excellent condition.

Good Condition

Minor scratch or scratches. Minor flaking. Minor fading. Possible minor dents. Little rust or pitting.

Fair Condition

Major scratch or scratches on surface. Picture or lettering faded. Rust spots on surface. Minor dent or dents. Bad chip or flaking on surface.

Poor Condition

Badly rusted, worn, dented, pitted, etc.

Victorian Girl
1897 – 9¼"
$10,000–12,000

Hilda Clark
1900 – 9¼"
$7,000–8,000

Hilda Clark
1899 – 9¼"
$8,500–11,000

Hilda Clark
1901 – 9¼"
$4,500–5,500

Pages 7 thru 27:
Trays must be in excellent condition.

Bottle Tray
1903 – 9¾"
$7,500–8,500+

Hilda Clark
1903 – 15x18½"
$6,000–7,000

Hilda Clark
1903 – 9¾"
$5,500–6,500

St. Louis Fair
1909 – 13½x16½"
$2,500–3,500

St. Louis Fair
1909 – 10¾x13"
$1,800–2,800

Lillian Nordica
1905 – 10½x13"
$3,000–4,000

Lillian Nordica
1905 – 10½x13"
$3,000–4,000

Juanita
1906 – 10½x13¼"
$2,000–2,750

Relieves Fatigue
1906 – 13¼x16¾"
$3,000–4,000

Relieves Fatigue
1907 – 10½x13¼"
$2,500–3,000

Topless
1908 – 12½"
$4,000–5,000

Coca–Cola™ Girl
1910 – 10½x13¼"
$800–1,000

1913 – 12½x15¼"
$650–850

1913 – 10½x13¼"
$600–800

Betty
1914 – 12½x15¼"
$600–850

Betty
1914 – 10½x13¼"
$500–750

Elaine
1916 – 8½x19"
$250–350

Warning: These four trays have been reproduced.

Garden Girl
1920 – 13¾x16½"
$800–1,000

Garden Girl
1920 – 10½x13¼"
$750–950

Summer Girl
1922 – 10½x13¼"
$800–900

Autumn Girl
1921 – 10½x13¼"
$750–850

Flapper Girl
1923 – 10½x13¼"
$400–500

Smiling Girl
1924 – 10½x13¼"
Maroon Rim – $800–900
Brown Rim – $650–750

Girl at Party
1925 – 10½x13⅛"
(reproduced in 1973)
$400–500

Sports Couple
1926 – 10½x13¼"
(reissued in 1974)
$700–800

Soda Jerk
1928 – 10½x13¼"
$650–850

Curb Service
1927 – 10½x13¼"
$650–850

Bobbed Hair Girl
1927 – 10½x13¼"
$600–700

Girl in Swimsuit Holding Glass
1929 – 10¼x13¼"
$400–500

Girl in Swimsuit Holding Bottle
1929 – 10½x13¼"
$500–600

Girl with Phone
1930 – 10½x13¼"
$350–450

Bathing Beauty
1930 – 10½x13¼"
$400–500

Boy with Dog
1931 – 10½x13¼"
$750–850

Girl on Bench
1932 – 10½x13¼"
$650–750

Francis Dee
1933 – 10½x13¼"
$500–600

Maureen O'Sullivan and Johnny Weismuller
1934 – 10½x13¼"
(warning – reproduced)
$800–1,000

Madge Evans
1935 – 10½x13¼"
$350–450

Hostess
1936 – 10½x13¼"
$300–400

Running Girl
1937 – 10½x13¼"
(reproduced)
$250–350

Girl in the Afternoon
1938 – 10½x13¼"
$225–325

Springboard Girl
1939 – 10½x13¼"
$250–350

Sailor Girl
1940 – 10½x13¼"
$225–325

Ice Skater
1940 – 10½x13¼"
$275–375

Roadster Girls
1941–1942 – 10½x13¼"
$325–425

Girl with Wind in Hair
1950 – 10½x13¼"
(reproduced)
$80–100

Girl with Menu
1955–1960 – 10½x13¼"
$45–65

Girl with Menu (French)
1955–1960 – 10½x13¼"
$85–100

TV Tray Assortment
1956 – 13½x18¾"
$10–20

Girl with Umbrella (Canadian)
1957 – 10½x13¼"
$225–325

*Left: Rooster Tray
(Canadian) – 1957
10½x13¼" – $125–225*

*Right: Bird House Tray
(Canadian) – 1957
10½x13¼" – $125–225*

*Above: Sandwich Tray (Canadian) – 1957 – 10½x14¼" – $125–225.
Right: Picnic Basket – 1958 – 10½x11¼" – $35–45*

*TV Tray Picnic Basket – 1958 – 13½x18¾"
$50–60*

*Pansy Garden – Be Really Refreshed – 1961 – 10½x13¼"
three variations – $15–25*

Pansy Garden, Coke™ Refreshes You Best
1961 – 10½x13¼"
(three variations)
$20–30

TV Tray, Thanksgiving
1961 – 13½x18¾"
$10–20

TV Tray, Candles
1961 – 13½x18¾"
$10–20

Duster Girl
1972 – 10¾x14¾"
$5

Lillian Nordica
Reproduction
1969 - 10¾x14¾″
$50-60

Lillian Nordica
Reproduction
1969 - 10¾x14¾″
$25-35

Lillian Nordica
Reproduction (French)
1968 - 10¾x14¾″
$40-50

Lillian Nordica
Reproduction (French)
1969 - 10¾x14¾″
$40-50

Left: Coca–Cola™ Girl
1910
1971 Reproduction
10¾x14¾" − $5

Right: Betty – 1972
1912 Reproduction
10½x13¾" − $15–25

Hamilton King (1914)
1972 reproduction
12½x15¼"
$15–20

Elaine (1916)
1972 reproduction
18½x19"
$15–20

1973 Christmas Tray
(many variations)
$10–20

Right: Calendar Girl (1927)
1974 reproduction
$20–25

Hilda Clark Change Tray
1900 – 6"
$2,500–3,500

Hilda Clark
Glass Change Receiver
1900 – 8½"
$4,000–5,000

Ceramic Change Receiver
1890s – 10½"
$3,500–4,500

Hilda Clark Change Tray
1901 – 6"
$2,000–3,000

Bottle Change Tray
1903 – 5½"
$5,000–6,000

Ceramic Change Receiver
1899 – 10½"
$5,000+

Hilda Clark Change Tray
1903 – 6"
$1,500–2,000

Griselda Change Receiver
1905 – 13x13"
$1,000–1,200

Hilda Clark Change Tray
1903 – 4"
$1,750–2,500

Juanita Change Tray
1906 – 4"
$650–750

Relieves Fatigue Change Tray
1907 – 4¼x6"
$650–750

St. Louis Fair Change Tray
1909 – 4¼x6"
$450–550

Coca–Cola™ Girl Change Tray
1910 – 4¼x6"
$450–550

Change Tray
1913 – 4¼x6"
$375–475

Betty Change Tray
1914 – 4¼x6"
$250–350

Elaine Change Tray
1916 – 4¼x6"
$150–250

Garden Girl Change Tray
1920 – 4¼x6"
$350–450

Glass Change Receiver
1907 – 7"
$1,000–1,200

1891
$10,000–12,000

1897
7⅜χ13"
$8,000–10,000

1898
cut from large calendar
$2,500+ as is

Part of 1899 Calendar – $1,000
if complete $8,000–10,000

1900
7¼χ12¾"
$8,000–10,000

1901 (wrong pad)
7⅝χ11"
$5,000–6,000

1900
$650–850

1901
7⅜χ13"
$4,500–5,500

1902 (wrong pad)
7½χ14½"
$5,000–6,000

1904 (with glass)
7¾χ15¼"
$3,500–4,500

1904 (with bottle)
7¾x15¼"
$3,500–4,500

1905
7¾x15¼"
$4,000–5,000

1906
7¾x15¼"
$3,500–4,500

1907
$5,000–6,000

1908 (top only)
7x14 – $1,500–1,800
if complete $3,500–4,500

1909
approx. 3¾x7¾"
$750–850
sometimes found with 1910
and 1911 calendar

1910
8¾x17½"
$4,000–5,000

1911
10½x17¼"
$3,500–4,500

1912 (wrong pad)
approx. 9¾x18"
$3,500–4,500
Large version – 12¼x30¾"
$5,000–6,000

1913
13½x22½"
$3,000–4,000

1914
13x32
$1,250–1,500

1915
13x32"
$2,500–3,000

1916 (wrong pad)
13x32"
$1,500–1,800

1917 – 13x32" – 2 versions
with glass – $2,500–3,000
wth bottle – $1,800–2,500

1918 (wrong pad)
13x32"
$3,000–3,500

1919 (wrong pad)
13x32"
$2,000–2,500

Marion Davis – 1919
6¼x10½"
$2,500–3,000

1920
12x32"
$1,800–2,500

1921
12x32"
$1,300–1,500

1922 (wrong pad)
12x32"
$1,800–2,200

1923
approx. 12x24"
$650–850

1924
12x24"
$1,000–1,250

1925
12x24"
$850–1,200

1926
10½x18½"
$1,200–1,500

1927
$900–1,200

1928
$900–1,200

1929
$1,000–1,250

1930
$1,000–1,250

1931
$750–850

1932
$500–600

Above calendars are approx. 12x24".

1933
$650–750

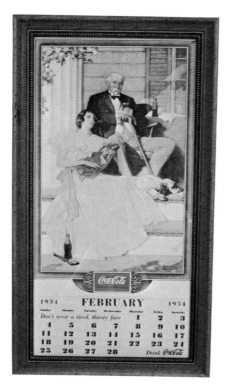

1934
$650–750

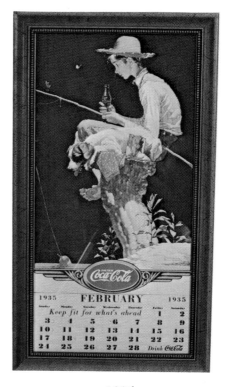

1935
$550–650
Warning: recently reproduced.

1936
$650–750

1937
$500–600

1938
$450–550

Above calendars are approx. 12x24".

1939 – 12x24"
$450–550

1972 – Cloth
$5–10

1973 – Cloth
$5–10

1973 Reproduction
of 1899 Calendar
$5–10

Desk Calendar – 1920s
$250–350

Hilda Clark Tin Sign
1899 – 20x28"
very rare
$15,000–18,000

Hilda Clark Tin Sign
1900 – 20x28"
extremely rare
$15,000–18,000

Bottle Tray Sign (tin)
1900–1903 – 8½x10⅛"
extremely rare
$7,000–8,000

Hilda Clark (tin)
1903 – 6" – extremely rare
$4,500–6,500

Distributor's
Sign – 1910 – $2,500–3,500

Hilda Clark (paper)
1901 – 15x20" – $6,500–7,500

Bottle Sign (celluloid)
1900–1910
6x13¼"
$1,500–1,800

Hilda Clark (tin)
1903 – 15x18½"
extremely rare
$4,500–6,500

Lillian Nordica
1904 – 8¼x10¼"
rare
$6,500–8,500

Lillian Nordica (tin)
1905 – 8¼x10¼"
$6,500–8,500

Lillian Nordica Cardboard Poster
1904 – 26x40"
$8,000–10,000

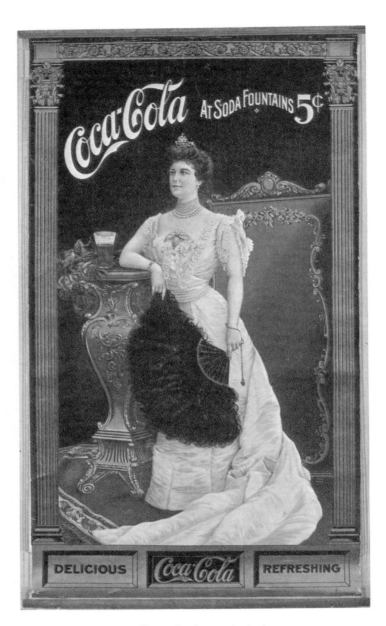

Lillian Nordica Oil Cloth
1904 – 25x47"
$8,000–10,000

Lillian Nordica Cameo Poster
1905 – 19x25"
$8,000–10,000

St. Louis Fair Cardboard Sign
1909 - 28x44" (trimmed)
$4,000 as is

Betty Tin Sign
1914 – 31x41"
$5,000–6,000

Elaine Tin Sign
1916 – 20x30"
$4,000–5,000

Gibson Girl Paper Sign
1910 – 20x30"
$4,000–5,000

Girl with Bottle Paper Sign
1913– 16x24"
$3,000–4,000

Paper Sign
1912 – 16x22"
$3,000–4,000

Paper Sign
1912 – 16x24"
$3,000–4,000

Glass Sign
1906 – 8" dia
blue w/gold trademark
$1,500–2,000

Glass Sign
1906 – 6¾x9"
maroon w/silver trademark
$1,500–2,000

Tin Sign – 1910–1912 – 27x19"
Beware of '70s reproduction trademark under Coca-Cola.
original – $1,000–1,250; reproduction – $350–450

Cardboard Sign – 1914
11x20½"
$3,000–4,000

Tin Sign – 1933
3' tall
$800–1,200

Cardboard Poster
1912
$3,500–4,500

Elaine Poster
1915
$2,000–3,000

Reverse glass – 1920s
6x10"
$1,000–1,200

Sign – 1926
8x11" – $2,000–2,500

Chrome – 1920's
17" – $475–575

Tin – 1926
8½x11"
$1,800–2,000

Festoon Sign – 1918
20x30" plus foldout
$4,000–5,000

Tin – 1927
8½x11"
$1,800–2,000

Tin Sign – 1927
30x7¾"
$550–750

Glass Sign – 1930s
11¼" dia
$500–600

Kaye Display – 1930s
wood
$1,000–1,250

Celluloid Sign – 1950s
9"
$150–200

Tin Sign – 1931
12½x4½"
$450–550

Art Plate/Western Coca–Cola™
Bottling Co.
1908–1912 – 10"
$650–750

Art Plate/Western Coca–Cola™
Bottling Co.
1908–1912 – 10"
$250–350

Note:
Prices listed are for art plates without ornate gold frames and/or shadow boxes.
Plates found with frames and/or shadow boxes could double in value.

Art Plate/Western Coca–Cola™
Bottling Co.
1908–1912 – 10"
$250–350

Art Plate/Western Coca–Cola™
Bottling Co.
1908–1912 – 10"
$250–350

Art Plate/Western Coca–Cola™
Bottling Co.
1908–1912 – 10"
$250–350

Art Plate/Western Coca–Cola™
Bottling Co.
1908–1912 – 10"
$250–350

Note:
Prices listed are for art plates without ornate gold frames and/or shadow boxes.
Plates found with frames and/or shadow boxes could double in value.

Art Plate – 10"
$250–370

Art Plate/Western Coca–Cola™
Bottling Co.
1908–1912 – 10"
$250–350

Art Plate/Western Coca–Cola™
Bottling Co.
1908–1912 – 10"
$350–450

Art Plate/Western Coca–Cola™
Bottling Co.
1908–1912 – 10"
$350–450

Note:
Prices listed are for art plates without ornate gold frames and/or shadow boxes.
Plates found with frames and/or shadow boxes could double in value.

E.M. Knowles China Co.
1930 – 7¼"
$250–350

Lenox China
1950 – 10½"
$300–400

1908 – 1¾χ2¾"
(reproduced)
$800–1,000

Juanita
1906 – 1¾χ2¾"
(reproduced) – $400–500

Relieves Fatigue
1907 – 1¾χ2¾"
$400–500

St. Louis Fair
1909 – 1¾χ2¾"
(reproduced)
$400–500

Coca–Cola™ *Girl*
1910 – 1¾χ2¾"
$225–325

Coca–Cola™ *Girl*
1911 – 1¾χ2¾"
(reproduced)
$225–325

1914 – 1¾χ2¾"
$450–550

Elaine
1916 – 1¾χ2¾"
(reproduced) – $300–400

1922 – 1¾χ2¾"
$1,400–1,600

Golden Girl
1920 – 1¾x2¾"
(reproduced)
$550–650

Pocket Mirror – 1936
$85–100

Fancy Mirror – 6'3"x4'
1970s – not company authorized
decorator value – not collectible

Metal Craft
1930s – 11"
$800–1,000

Marx Sprite Boy – 1940s
$450–650

Marx Sprite Boy Stake – 1940s
$425–625

Marx No. 21 – 1950s
$350–450

Japan Tin – 4" – 1950s
$125–175

Matchbox – 2" – 1960s
even load
$50–65

Budgie Truck – 5" – 1950s
$325–425

Matchbox – 2" – 1960s
staggered load
$100–125

Japan Tin – 4" – 1950s
$125–150

Barclay
Late 1950s – 2"
$125–175

Marvsan Truck (Japan)
1950s – 8"
$750–850

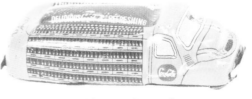

Buddy–L – 1960s
yellow bumper
$300–400

Sanyo Japan – 1960s
$250–350
red version
350–450

Linemar (Japan)
1950s – 2¾"
$175–225

Wiking (Germany)
1970s – 1¾"
$50–75

Taiyo VW (Japan) – 1960s
$250–350

Plastic w/insert
1960s — 4½"
rare
$125–175

1964 — 4½"
rare version — $125–145
recent version — $25–35

V–W (Japan) — 1950s
$225–325

Winross
1974 — 9½"
(3 rear door variations)
$125–150

Buddy–L — 1974
$65–85 — near mint

Corgie, Jr
1974 — 3"
$10–12

Big Wheels — 1970s
(3 variations)
$80–100

Vending Machine – Model Kit
Plastic – 1960s – 5"
$80–100

Ford Station Wagon (Japan)
1960s – 5"
very rare
$1,250–1,450

Taiyo Ford Sedan (Japan) – 1960s
$225–275

Buddy–L Can Car – 1970s
$50–60

Lionel Train Set – 1974
with box $350–450

Toy Stove – 1930s
$1,500–2,500

American Flyer – 1930s
$1,250–1,750

Marbles – 1950s
$40–50

Linemar Dispenser (Japan) – 1950s
$500–600

Jigsaw Puzzle in Can
1968–1969
$45–65

Russell Yo–Yo – 1960s
$15–25

Tin Whistle
1930s
$100–125

Bean Bag – 1971
$15–20

Tin Bank – 1950s
$100–125

Bank
1950s – 5½"
$125–145

Can Bank – 1960s
$25–35

Oak Barrel
Bank – 6"
$35–45

Cap Bank – 1960s
$15–25

Checkers – 1940s
(each piece marked Coca–Cola™)
$40–50

Dominos – 1940s
(each piece marked Coca–Cola™)
$40–60

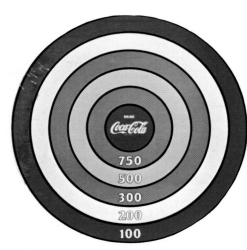

Dart Board – 1950s
$65–85

Table Tennis Paddles – 1950s
$40–50 each; $250–350 full set

Boomerang
1950s
$15–20

Model Plane – 1960s
$35–40

Frisbee – 1960s
$15–20

Tic–Tac–Toe – 1950s
$100–125

Bang Gun – 1960s
$40–50

Magic Kit – 1965
$125–175

Comic Book – 1951
$20–25

Cribbage Board – 1940s
$25–35

Handkerchief – 1953
22x20"
$75–85
reproduced in 1985
white $20–25

American Flyer
Kite – 1930s
$300–400

Bingo Card – 1930
$30–40

Bingo Card – 1950s
$6–8

Wire Puzzle – 1960s
$25–35

Biedenharn
pre–1902
$225–325

Script
Hutchinson
ca. 1900
$1,250–1,750

Biedenharn
ca. 1905
with label
$150–175

Biedenharn
Candy
ca. 1905
$125–175

Miniature Perfume
1930s
beware of reproductions
$50–75

Display Bottle
1923 – 20"
with cap – $300–350
Pat. D – $350–450

For Toy
Cooler
1951 – 3½"
$15–20

Monsanto
Experimental
1960s – $35–45
found in several colors

Seltzer
Billings, Mont.
$350–450

Blue Seltzer
$150–200

Blue Seltzer
$150–200

Syrup – 1900s
$550–750

Glass Label
Syrup – 1900s
$550–750

Blue Syrup
1920s
$750–850

Clear Syrup
1920s
$400–500

Syrup – 1910
$650–850

1965 Root Commemorative (gold clasp) – $400–500
1971 Root Commemorative (silver clasp) – $275–350

1974–75th Anniversary
Thomas Bottling Company
$60–75
Prices will vary depending on manufacturer.

Miami
Technical
1961
$150–200

1974
75th Anniversary
Chattanooga
$5–10

Six Bottle Carrier – 1924
$225–275

Six Bottle Carrier – 1930s – $65–75

Six Bottle Carrier – 1930s
$75–95

Vendor's Carrier – 1950s
$175–225

Left: Six Bottle
Carrier – 1940s
$125–150

Right: Six Bottle
Carrier – 1940s
$125–150

48 Bottle Shipping Case
1918
9x18x25½"
$250–350

Plastic Bottles & Case – 1970s
$15–20

Miniature 6 Pack – 1970s
(plastic bottles)
$3–5

Box of 4–1 gallon bottles – 1920s
set $450–550; bottle $100

Miniature Plastic Carrying Case
1970s
$3–5

Embossed Bottles & Case – 1920s – $100–150

Miniature 6 Pack – 1970s
(gold metal bottles)
$3–5

Plastic Bottles & Case – 1960s
$25–35

Glass Holder – 1890s – $1,000–1,250
1973 reproduction $15; 1990 reproduction $5

Note: "Drink" does not
appear on original
←

Bottle Holder – 1950s – $25–35

Car Window
Holder – 1940s
$65–85

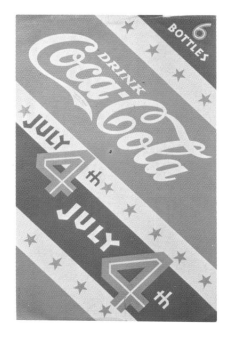

Carton Wrapper – 1930s
$250–350

Car Window Holder 1950s
$15–25

Miniature Sales Aid – 1950s
$175–225

Metal 6 Bottle Carrier – 1950s
$65–85

*Salesman's Sample
of a 1928 Glascock Cooler
13x10½x8"
$6,500–7,500*

*Salesman's Samples of a 1939 Cooler
8½x11x9"
$2,500–3,500*

*Salesman's Sample of a 1939 Cooler
8½x11x9"
$2,800–3,800
complete w/carrying case $3,000–4,000*

*Mengel – Bottle Ice Cooler – 1920s – 32x38"
$1,200–1,500*

Leaded Glass Shade, 18" – ca. 1920s – $3,500–4,500

Note:
Must read:
Property of the
Coca-Cola Co.
to be returned
on demand.
←

Leaded Glass Fixture – ca. 1910
22x11x7½" – $10,000+

Leaded Glass Globe – 1920s – $7,500–10,000

Milk Glass Light Shade
1930s – 14" – $800–1,000

Milk Glass Light Fixture
1930s – 10"
$1,250–1,750

Bottle Lamp, 20" – 1920s
$6,500–7,500

Hilda Clark Celluloid Desk Clock
1901 — 7¾x5½"
extremely rare
$7,500–8,500

Baird Clock Co. — 1896–1899
15 day movement
$6,500–7,500

Baird Clock Co. — 1891–1895
Ideal Brain Tonic
$4,000–6,000

Gilbert – 1910
40x18" – $4,000–5,000

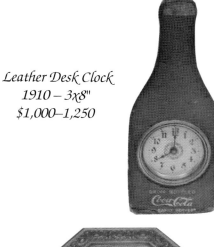

Leather Desk Clock
1910 – 3x8"
$1,000–1,250

1972 Plastic Reissue
$50–60

Gilbert – 1916–1920
beware of reproductions
$1,000–1,250

Leather Desk Clock
1910 – 4½x6"
$1,000–1,250

1974 Plastic
$50–60

Dome Clock – 1950
3x5"
$650–750

Dome Clock – 1950s
6x9", reproduced
$1,000–1,200

Early 1900s
5x21" – wood
$375–475

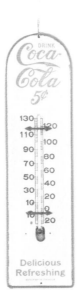

1905 – Wood
4x15"
$350–450

1950s – 2¼x7½"
$15–20

1941 – 7x16"
$250–350

1939 – 6½x16"
$250–350

1930s – Tin
$275–375

Flare – ca. 1912
$350–450

1912–1916
$300–350

5¢ – ca. 1912–1913
$750–850

Swedish Glass Plate – 1969
8¼x6¼" – $80–100

Modified Flare
1923–1927
$100–125

1935 Trademark – $35–45

Pewter – 1930s
$350–450
w/leather pouch
$650–750

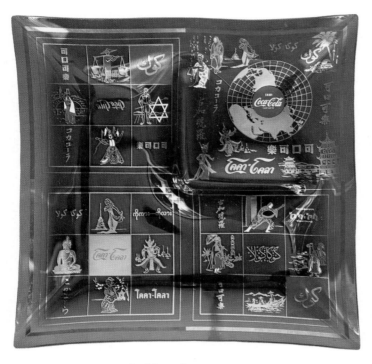

World Dish (square) – 1967
11½x11½"
$85–100

Leaded Glass Bottle
1920s – 36" tall
extremely rare
$12,000–15,000

World Dish (round) – 1967 – 7"
$85–100

Shipping Case – 1913 – 12½x6¼"
$450–650

Display Box – 1920s
$1,250–1,750

Cylindrical Gum – 1903–1905
$750–850

Bookmark – 1904
(framed)
$1,000–1,250
very rare

Bookmark – 1904
$1,000–1,200
very rare

Shipping Box – 1916
$750–850

Franklin–Caro Co.–1915
$100–125

Coca–Cola™ Pepsin 1905–1910
$1,000–1,200

Crown Top – 1903–1905
$800–1,000

Adv. Top – 1905–1910
$800–1,000

Gum Wrapper (framed) – 1916–1920
$400–500

Wrapper – 1911–1913
$400–500

Advertisement – 1904
$150–200

Fan – 1912–1916
$1,500–2,500

Wrapper (Pepsin) – 1916–1920
$400–500

Advertisement – 1905
$150–200

Wrapper (Spearmint) – 1916–1920
$400–500

Gold Wash & Silver
1907 – 1¾x1½"
$100–150; sterling 250–300

Bottle – 1905
1¾x1¼"
$800–1,000

Coca–Cola™ Bottling Co.
Memphis, TN
1910 – 1¾x1½"
$175–225

Drink Coca–Cola™ in Bottles 5¢
1911 – 1½x2"
$650–750

Girl & Bottle – 1910
1¾x1¼"
$750–850

Brass w/Black Enamel
1912 – 1½x1¼"
$150–200

Celluloid – 1912 – 1½"
$1,500–1,750

Type I – 1920s
1½x1"
$125–175

Type II – 1920s
1¾x1¼"
$125–175

Rectangle – 1920s
1½x1¼"
$150–175

Drink Coca–Cola™ in Bottles
(on back)
1½x1¼", $150–175
1909 Convention Coca-Cola
Bottlers Atlanta
(on back)
$500–600

Indian Design – 1920s
$150–250

Fantasy!
Ca. 1908 – 1¾x1½"
(could be from 1960s or 70s)
$25

*1905–1915 Warning: Many reproductions. Blade must be
marked Kaster & Co. Coca-Cola Bottling Co., Germany
$350–400*

*Try a Bottle
1910
$275–325*

*Bone Handle Combination – 1915–1925
$100–150*

*Combination Henry
Sears & Son
'Solingen'
1920s
$350–405*

*The Coca–Cola™ Bottling Co. – 1940s
$40–50*

*Compliments – The Coca–Cola™ Co.
1930s
$60–75*

*Serve Coca–Cola™
1940s
$150–200*

*Switchblade Remington – 1930s
$200–250*

*Drink Coca–Cola™ in Bottles – 1940s
$75–85*

Cast Iron (block print)
1900–1920
$100–125

Legs Opener ca. 1920
$150–200

1930s Drink Coca–Cola™ in
Sterilized Bottles
$75

Brass Key – 1910–1920
$60–80

Saber
1920s–1930s
$150–200

1920s–1950s
$15–20

Drink Coca–Cola™
1909–1950s
$5–20

Spoon & Opener – 1930s
$75–100

1930s
$35–45

Bottle Shape – 1950s
$100–125

Flat Opener – 1950s
$35–45

50th Anniversary
Nashville, TN – 1952
$60–80
gold plated

Have a Coke™
1950s & 60s
$5

Drink Coca–Cola™ in
Bottles – 1920s & 1940s
$15

Beer Type
$5

Ice Pick & Opener – 1940s
$10–15

Crosley Bottle Radio – 1930s
30"
$4,500–6,500

Cooler Radio – 1950s
$800–1,000

Crystal Radio – 1950s – 2¾"
$250–350

Music Box – 1950s
(many variations of songs)
$125–175

1963 – 7½x3½"
$150–175

1960s – 4½x2½"
$300–400

Transistor Radio
1970s
$125–175

Can Radio – 1970s
$20–30

1906 Sheet Music – Songs Include: "My Old Kentucky Home," "The Palms," "Rock Me To Sleep Mother," "Old Folks at Home," "Juanita," "Lead Kindly Light," "Nearer, My God to Thee," "We Found That He'd Been Drinking Coca–Cola™," "Ben Bolt," "My Coca–Cola™ Bride." $750–850 each, except Juanita – $1,000–2,000

"*The Coca–Cola*™ *Girl*" – 1927
9½x12½"
$250–350

Song Sheet – 1969
"*It's the Real Thing*"
$5–10

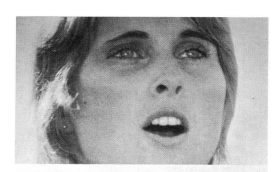

"*I'd Like to Buy the World a Coke*™" – 1971 – 8¾x11¼"
$20–25

Lone Ranger – 1971
Record Jacket – $25–30

Dick Tracy – 1971
Record Jacket – $25–30

Superman – 1971
Record Jacket – $25–30

Sgt. Preston of the Yukon – 1971
Record Jacket – $25–30

Salesman Training Records
1940s–1950s
33⅓ – $12–15

W.C. Fields – 1971
Record Jacket – $25–30

Tony Bennett – 1951
$10–12

"It's the Real Thing" – 1971
$2–5

1907 Matchbook Holder – $225–325

1907 Matchbook Holder – $225–325

*Celluloid Matchbook
Holder – 1910
$250–275*

*Pullmatch Ash Tray – 1940s
$1,000–1,200*

*Cigarette Box – 1936
$650–750*

*Match Safe – 1908
$450–550*

Cigar Band – 1930s – $100–125

*Musical Lighter
1963
$125–175*

*Bakelite Lighter 1950s
$15–18
(beware of reproductions)*

*Miniature Lighter
1960s – 1½"
$35–45*

*Can Lighter
1960s
$20–25*

Brass 50th Anniversary – 1936
$50–75

Ruby Glass Ash Trays – 1950s
$425–500 set w/box – $80–100 each

Bottle Ash Tray
Bills Novelties – 1950
$125–150

Things Go Better w/Coke™ – 1960s
$5–8

Drink Coca–Cola™ – 1960s
$5

Drink Coca–Cola™ – 1950s
$5–8

Engraved Coin Purse – 1907
$125–175

Embossed Coin Purse – 1907
$150–175

Wallet – 1907
$85–100

Left: Coin Purse – 1910 – $150–175
Right: Coin Purse – 1920s – $125–175

Wallet - 1920's - $20-30

Wallet - 1915 - $60-80

Wallet - 1920's - $20-30

LEFT: Wallet w/Calendar - 1918 - $60-80

Wallet w/calendar - 1920's - $60-80

Bottle Wallet - 1920's - $25-35

Wallet - 1960's - $15-20

"The Romance of Coca–Cola™" – 1916 – $75–85

"Facts" – 1923
$50–60

"Alphabet Book of Coca–Cola™" – 1928
$50–60

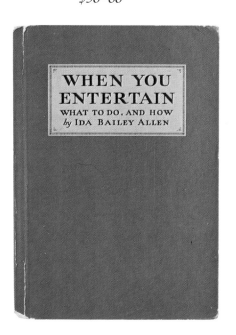

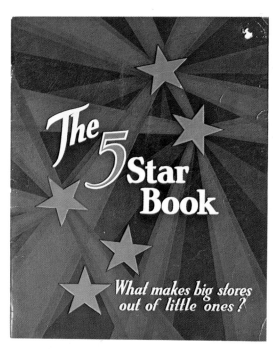

"The 5 Star Book" – 1928
$30–40

"When You Entertain" – 1932 – $10–15

"The Red Barrel" – 1940s – $12–15 each

"Know Your War Planes" – 1940s – $40–50

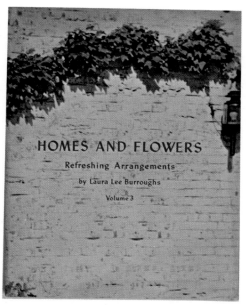

"Homes and Flowers"
1940s
$8–10

"The Coca–Cola™ Bottler"
1944
$20–25

"My Daily Reminder" – 1939 – $12–15

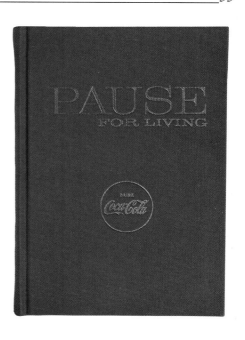

Left:
"Easy Hospitality" – 1951
$6–8

Right:
"Pause for Living" (bound) –1961
$10–15

"Pause for Living"
(single copies)
$2–5 each

Left:
"Flower Arranging"
1940s – $8–10

Right:
"Flower Arranging II"
1940s – $8–10

Hall of Fame Records – 1960 – $50–60

Bat – 1950s
$150–200

Scorekeeper – 1907
$80–100

Glove – 1920s – $225–325

Miniature Ball – 1960 's
$5–10

Miniature Ball – 1960s
$10–12

Score Pad – 1940s
$8–10

Popcorn Container
& Megaphone
1960s – $10–15

Celluloid Pencil Holder – 1910
$125–150

Baseball Bat Pen – 1940s
$40–50

Mechanical Pencil – 1930s
$20–25

Pen – 1950s
$45–65

School Set – 1930s
$50–75

Round Pencil Sharpener
1960
$8–10

Rectangular Pencil
Sharpener – 1960s
$8–10

Bottle Pencil
Sharpener – 1930s
$30–40

Pledge Pin
$25–30

5 Year Pin
$65–75

10 Year Pin
$50–75

15 Year Pin
$50–75

20 Year Pin
$50–75

30 Year Pin – $100–125

50 Year Pin
$250–350+ extremely rare

Convention Pin – 1912
$500–600

Convention Badge – 1915
$500–600

Driver's Hat Pin – 1930 – 4" long
$175–200

Convention Pin – 1916 – $500–600

Commemorative 50–Dollar Gold Coin
1970s
gold value +

5¢ Token – 1930s
$10–15

Commemorative Silver Ingot – 1970s
$20–25

Coca–Cola™ Girl – Hamilton King – 1910
$625–725

Motor Girl – 1911
5½x3½"
$625–725

1910 – 5½x3½"
$125

Delivery Wagon – 1913
$125

Bottling Plant – 1905
$125

Delivery Wagon – 1900
$125

1915 – 5½x3½"

Bottling Plant – 1910

Delivery Auto Truck – 1913

Bottling Plant – 1906

Bottling Plant – 1909

Delivery Truck – 1910

Store – 1904

*Pictorial Post Cards 1900–1920
$125–175 each*

Store – 1904

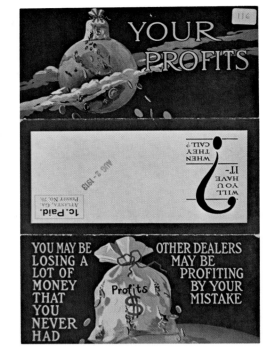

Folding Postal Cards – ca. 1910–1920
$400–500 each

1909 – $2,000–2,500 complete boxed set

1915 – $1,500–1,750 complete boxed set

1943 – $80–100 boxed set

1928 – $400–500 boxed set

1956 – $60–80 boxed set

1963 – $50–60 boxed set

1961 – $50–60 boxed set

1911
$150–200

1920s
$50–60

1915
$65–85

1930s
$45–65

1930s
$45–65

1950s
$25–35

1904 Chicago $100–125
Atlanta $375–425

1904
$350–450

1905
$200–250

1913
$30–40

1916
$35–45

1913
$25–35

1929
$75–85

1929
$100–150

1930
$50–60

Blotters – 1970s
Full Set $250–350

(front)

(back)

Confederate Bank Note Souvenir – 1931
$60–80

(front)

(back)

Hilda Clark Menu – 1903
4⅛x6⅛"
$600–700

Hilda Clark Menu – 1901 – very rare
11¾x4" – $1,200–1,500

Lillian Nordica Menu – 1904
4⅛x6½"
$600–700

(front)

(back)

Opera Program – 1906
$80–100

Soda Menu – 1902
4⅛x6⅛" – $600–700

Magic Lantern Pictures (all hand colored glass) – 1920s
$125–150 each

(front)

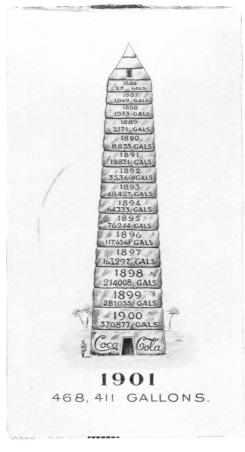

(back)

Celluloid Note Pad – 1902 – 2½x5"
$550–650

Note Pad – 1905 – 2¾x4½"
$225–325

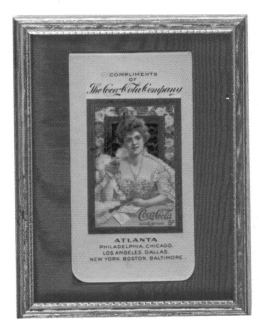

Hilda Clark Note Pad – 1903 – 5x2½"
$500–600

Left: Writing Pad
1960s – $5–6

Right: Writing Pad
1950s – $5–6

Writing Pad – 1960s – $5–6

Pocket Secretary – 1920s
$25–35

Sugar Ration Book – 1943
$35–40

Advertiser (Miniature) – 1929
$100–125

Letterhead – 1887
$150–200

Asa G. Candler Letter – 1889
$150–200

Asa G. Candler – 1889
$175–250

Invoices – 1900, 1903
$80–100

Needle Case – 1924
$65–85

Needle Case – 1925
$65–85

(open)

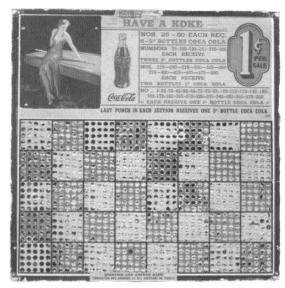

Punch Board – 1930s – 9¼x9¼"
rare – $500–600

Punch Board – 1930s – 9¼x9¼"
rare – $500–600

Nature Study Cards – 1930s
$8–12 pack
$85–125 set of 12

American Fighting Planes – 1943
$125–135 full set
with original envelope

Cherub – 14¾"
$3,500–4,500

Comic Trade Card – 1905
Beware of reproductions – $750–850

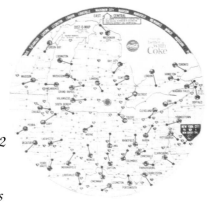

(open)

Book Jacket – 1925
$45–65

Bottle Bags – 1930s & 1940s – $3–5 each

Left Olympiad Records – 1932
$100–125

Right: Mileage Table – 1950s
$50–60

Bookmark – 1896 – 2x2¼"
$850–1,050

(back)

Celluloid Bookmark – 1899 – 2x2¼"
$500–600

Celluloid Hilda Clark
Bookmark – 1898
$600–700

Celluloid Hilda Clark
Bookmark – 1900
$500–600

Hilda Clark
Bookmark – 1903
$375–475

Bookmark – 1903
$1,000–1,200
Rare

Lillian Nordica
Bookmark – 1904
$325–425

Lillian Nordica
Bookmark – 1905
$475–575

Bookmark (celluloid) – 1906
$650–750

(front)   *Hilda Clark Coupon, 1⅝x3⅜" – 1901 – $500–550*   *(back)*

Coupon – 1890s – 1½x3⅜"
$225–275

Coupon – 1903 – 1⅝x3⅜"
$375–425

Lillian Nordica Coupon, 6½x9¾", 1905 – $200–250

Coupon – 1908 – 1⅝x3⅜"
$150–200

Letter & Coupon – 1900
$400–500

Coupon – 1920s – 2x5"
$25–35

Coupon – 1920s
$8–10

Coupon – 1920s
$10–15

Coupon – 1930s
$5–15

Coupon – 1920s
$10–15

Soda Jerk Coupon
1927 – 2¼x4"
$65–85

Coupon – 1950s
$4–5

Coupon – 1950s
$8–10

Fountain Seat
1900s
$250–350
rare

Bench – 1900s
$1,000–1,200

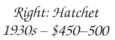

Left: Binoculars
1910 – $450–500

Right: Hatchet
1930s – $450–500

Bell – 1920s
$375–425

Safety Marker – 1920s
$125–175

Door Knobs – 1915
$350–450

Door Lock – 1920s
$65–85

Toaster – 1920s – very rare – $1,000–1,250

Bowl – 1930s – $350–400

Aluminum Pretzel Dish – 1930s – $175–200

Silverware – 1920s – $125–175 each piece

Potato Peeler – 1950s – $80–100

*Salt & Pepper Shakers – 1920s
$325–375*

*Perfume Bottle & Sterling Silver
Holder – 1960s
$325–375*

Delivery Wagon Umbrella – 1913
$1,000–1,200

Distributor's Calendar – 1918
with full pad – $350–400

Calendar Hanger – 1950s
$5–10

Plastic & Metal
Door Push
1950s
$150–225
beware of
reproductions

Door Push – 1930s
$375–425 complete w/iron bar

Night Light – 1950s
$80–100

Aluminum Thimble
1920s – $25–35

(small shown)

Wall Sconce – 1930
small – $325–375
large – 500–550

Also available with "Marines," "Coast Guard" same price.

Army Sewing Kit – 1940s
$50–60

Navy Sewing Kit – 1940s – $50–60

O.P.A. Token Holder – 1943
$60–75

(open)

Convention Hat – 1937 – $175–225

Car Plate – 1950s – $25–35

Car Plate – 1960s – $20–25

Pillow – 1950s – $60–80

Magnifying Glass – 1950s
$15–20

First Aid Kit – 1950s
$25–35

Mileage Table – 1950s
$1,000–1,250

Golf Tee Set – 1950s
$10

Pocket Comb – 1950s
$3–5

Plastic Place Mats – 1970s
$10–20 set

Ice Cream Container
"A Float w/Coke™" – 1950s
$10–15
must be in original package

Syrup Can – 1930s
$325–375

Santa Claus – 1950s, Rushton, Atl. GA –
$100–125 w/white boots, $125–175, w/black boots

Buddy Lee Doll – 1940s–1950s
$650 composition/$375 plastic

Miniature Bisque Dispenser
Pencil Holder – 1960s
$275–325

4 pc Syrup Dispenser 1890s Marked "Wheeling Pottery Co."
$4,500–6,500 if complete and in excellent condition

Sales Promotion Car Key – 1950s
$50–60

Left: Key Chain
1955 – $35–45

Right: Caps
$25–35 each

BOOKS ON COLLECTIBLES

This is only a partial listing of the books on antiques that are available from Collector Books. All books are well illustrated and contain current values. Most of the following books are available from your local bookseller, antique dealer, or public library. If you are unable to locate certain titles in your area, you may order by mail from COLLECTOR BOOKS, P.O. Box 3009, Paducah, KY 42002-3009. Customers with Visa or MasterCard may phone in orders from 7:00–4:00 CST, Monday–Friday, Toll Free 1-800-626-5420. Add $2.00 for postage for the first book ordered and $0.30 for each additional book. Include item number, title, and price when ordering. Allow 14 to 21 days for delivery.

DOLLS, FIGURES & TEDDY BEARS

2382	**Advertising Dolls**, Identification & Values, Robison & Sellers	$9.95
2079	**Barbie** Doll Fashions, Volume I, Eames	$24.95
3957	**Barbie** Exclusives, Rana	$18.95
3310	**Black Dolls**, 1820–1991, Perkins	$17.95
3873	**Black Dolls**, Book II, Perkins	$17.95
3810	**Chatty Cathy** Dolls, Lewis	$15.95
2021	Collector's **Male Action Figures**, Manos	$14.95
1529	Collector's Encyclopedia of **Barbie** Dolls, DeWein	$19.95
3727	Collector's **Guide to Ideal Dolls**, Izen	$18.95
3728	Collector's Guide to Miniature **Teddy Bears**, Powell	$17.95
4506	**Dolls in Uniform**, Bourgeois	$18.95
3967	Collector's Guide to **Trolls**, Peterson	$19.95
1067	**Madame Alexander** Dolls, Smith	$19.95
3971	**Madame Alexander** Dolls Price Guide #20, Smith	$9.95
2185	**Modern Collector's** Dolls I, Smith	$17.95
2186	**Modern Collector's** Dolls II, Smith	$17.95
2187	**Modern Collector's** Dolls III, Smith	$17.95
2188	**Modern Collector's** Dolls IV, Smith	$17.95
2189	**Modern Collector's** Dolls V, Smith	$17.95
3733	**Modern Collector's** Dolls, Sixth Series, Smith	$24.95
3991	**Modern Collector's** Dolls, Seventh Series, Smith	$24.95
3472	**Modern Collector's** Dolls Update, Smith	$9.95
3972	Patricia Smith's **Doll Values**, Antique to Modern, 11th Edition	$12.95
3826	Story of **Barbie**, Westenhouser	$19.95
1513	**Teddy Bears & Steiff** Animals, Mandel	$9.95
1817	**Teddy Bears & Steiff** Animals, 2nd Series, Mandel	$19.95
2084	**Teddy Bears, Annalee's & Steiff** Animals, 3rd Series, Mandel	$19.95
1808	Wonder of **Barbie**, Manos	$9.95
1430	World of **Barbie** Dolls, Manos	$9.95

TOYS, MARBLES & CHRISTMAS COLLECTIBLES

3427	**Advertising Character** Collectibles, Dotz	$17.95
2333	Antique & Collector's **Marbles**, 3rd Ed., Grist	$9.95
3827	Antique & Collector's **Toys**, 1870–1950, Longest	$24.95
3956	Baby Boomer **Games**, Identification & Value Guide, Polizzi	$24.95
1514	**Character Toys** & Collectibles, Longest	$19.95
1750	**Character Toys** & Collector's, 2nd Series, Longest	$19.95
3717	**Christmas** Collectibles, 2nd Edition, Whitmyer	$24.95
1752	**Christmas** Ornaments, Lights & Decorations, Johnson	$19.95
3874	Collectible Coca-Cola Toy **Trucks**, deCourtivron	$24.95
2338	Collector's Encyclopedia of **Disneyana**, Longest, Stern	$24.95
2151	Collector's Guide to **Tootsietoys**, Richter	$16.95
3436	Grist's Big Book of **Marbles**	$19.95
3970	Grist's Machine-Made & Contemporary **Marbles**, 2nd Ed.	$9.95
3732	**Matchbox®** Toys, 1948 to 1993, Johnson	$18.95
3823	**Mego** Toys, An Illustrated Value Guide, Chrouch	15.95
1540	**Modern Toys** 1930–1980, Baker	$19.95
3888	**Motorcycle** Toys, Antique & Contemporary, Gentry/Downs	$18.95
3891	Schroeder's Collectible **Toys**, Antique to Modern Price Guide	$17.95
1886	Stern's Guide to **Disney** Collectibles	$14.95
2139	Stern's Guide to **Disney** Collectibles, 2nd Series	$14.95
3975	Stern's Guide to **Disney** Collectibles, 3rd Series	$18.95
2028	**Toys**, Antique & Collectible, Longest	$14.95
3975	**Zany Characters** of the Ad World, Lamphier	$16.95

JEWELRY, HATPINS, WATCHES & PURSES

1712	Antique & Collector's **Thimbles** & Accessories, Mathis	$19.95
1748	Antique **Purses**, Revised Second Ed., Holiner	$19.95
1278	Art Nouveau & Art Deco **Jewelry**, Baker	$9.95
3875	Collecting Antique **Stickpins**, Kerins	$16.95
3722	Collector's Ency. of **Compacts, Carryalls & Face Powder Boxes**, Mueller	$24.95
3992	Complete Price Guide to **Watches**, #15, Shugart	$21.95
1716	Fifty Years of Collector's **Fashion Jewelry**, 1925-1975, Baker	$19.95
1424	**Hatpins** & Hatpin Holders, Baker	$9.95
1181	100 Years of Collectible **Jewelry**, Baker	$9.95
2348	20th Century Fashionable Plastic **Jewelry**, Baker	$19.95
3830	Vintage **Vanity Bags & Purses**, Gerson	$24.95

FURNITURE

1457	American **Oak** Furniture, McNerney	$9.95
3716	American **Oak** Furniture, Book II, McNerney	$12.95
1118	Antique **Oak** Furniture, Hill	$7.95
2132	Collector's Encyclopedia of **American** Furniture, Vol. I, Swedberg	$24.95
2271	Collector's Encyclopedia of **American** Furniture, Vol. II, Swedberg	$24.95
3720	Collector's Encyclopedia of **American** Furniture, Vol. III, Swedberg	$24.95
1437	Collector's Guide to **Country** Furniture, Raycraft	$9.95
3878	Collector's Guide to **Oak** Furniture, George	$12.95
1755	Furniture of the **Depression Era**, Swedberg	$19.95
3906	**Heywood-Wakefield** Modern Furniture, Rouland	$18.95
1965	**Pine** Furniture, Our American Heritage, McNerney	$14.95
1885	**Victorian** Furniture, Our American Heritage, McNerney	$9.95
3829	**Victorian** Furniture, Our American Heritage, Book II, McNerney	$9.95
3869	**Victorian** Furniture books, 2 volume set, McNerney	$19.90

INDIANS, GUNS, KNIVES, TOOLS, PRIMITIVES

1868	Antique **Tools**, Our American Heritage, McNerney	$9.95
2015	Archaic **Indian** Points & Knives, Edler	$14.95
1426	**Arrowheads** & Projectile Points, Hothem	$7.95
1668	**Flint Blades** & Projectile Points of the North American Indian, Tully	$24.95
2279	**Indian** Artifacts of the Midwest, Hothem	$14.95
3885	**Indian** Artifacts of the Midwest, Book II, Hothem	$16.95
1964	**Indian** Axes & Related Stone Artifacts, Hothem	$14.95
2023	**Keen Kutter** Collectibles, Heuring	$14.95
3887	Modern **Guns**, Identification & Values, 10th Ed., Quertermous	$12.95
2164	**Primitives**, Our American Heritage, McNerney	$9.95
1759	**Primitives**, Our American Heritage, Series II, McNerney	$14.95
3325	Standard **Knife** Collector's Guide, 2nd Ed., Ritchie & Stewart	$12.95

PAPER COLLECTIBLES & BOOKS

1441	Collector's Guide to **Post Cards**, Wood	$9.95
2081	Guide to Collecting **Cookbooks**, Allen	$14.95
3969	Huxford's **Old Book** Value Guide, 7th Ed.	$19.95
3821	Huxford's **Paperback** Value Guide	$19.95
2080	Price Guide to **Cookbooks & Recipe Leaflets**, Dickinson	$9.95
2346	**Sheet Music** Reference & Price Guide, Pafik & Guiheen	$18.95

OTHER COLLECTIBLES

2280	Advertising **Playing Cards**, Grist	$16.95
2269	Antique **Brass & Copper** Collectibles, Gaston	$16.95
1880	Antique **Iron**, McNerney	$9.95
3872	Antique **Tins**, Dodge	$24.95
1714	**Black** Collectibles, Gibbs	$19.95
1128	**Bottle** Pricing Guide, 3rd Ed., Cleveland	$7.95
3959	**Cereal Box** Bonanza, The 1950's, Bruce	$19.95
3718	Collector's **Aluminum**, Grist	$16.95
3445	Collectible **Cats**, An Identification & Value Guide, Fyke	$18.95
1634	Collector's Ency. of Figural & Novelty **Salt & Pepper Shakers**, Davern	$19.95
2020	Collector's Ency. of Figural & Novelty **Salt & Pepper Shakers**, Vol. II, Davern	$19.95
2018	Collector's Encyclopedia of **Granite Ware**, Greguire	$24.95
3430	Collector's Encyclopedia of **Granite Ware**, Book II, Greguire	$24.95
3879	Collector's Guide to Antique **Radios**, 3rd Ed., Bunis	$18.95
1916	Collector's Guide to **Art Deco**, Gaston	$14.95
3880	Collector's Guide to **Cigarette Lighters**, Flanagan	$17.95
1537	Collector's Guide to **Country Baskets**, Raycraft	$9.95
3966	Collector's Guide to **Inkwells**, Identification & Values, Badders	$18.95
3881	Collector's Guide to **Novelty Radios**, Bunis/Breed	$18.95
3729	Collector's Guide to **Snow Domes**, Guarnaccia	$18.95
3730	Collector's Guide to **Transistor Radios**, Bunis	$15.95
2276	**Decoys**, Kangas	$24.95
1629	**Doorstops**, Identification & Values, Bertoia	$9.95
3968	**Fishing Lure** Collectibles, Murphy/Edmisten	$24.95
3817	**Flea Market Trader**, 9th Ed., Huxford	$12.95
3819	**General Store Collectibles**, Wilson	$24.95
2215	Goldstein's **Coca-Cola** Collectibles	$16.95
3884	Huxford's **Collector's Advertising**, 2nd Ed.	$24.95
2216	**Kitchen Antiques**, 1790–1940, McNerney	$14.95
1782	1,000 **Fruit Jars**, 5th Edition, Schroeder	$5.95
3321	Ornamental & Figural **Nutcrackers**, Rittenhouse	$16.95
2026	**Railroad** Collectibles, 4th Ed., Baker	$14.95
1632	**Salt & Pepper Shakers**, Guarnaccia	$9.95
1888	**Salt & Pepper Shakers** II, Identification & Value Guide, Book II, Guarnaccia	$14.95
2220	**Salt & Pepper Shakers** III, Guarnaccia	$14.95
3443	**Salt & Pepper Shakers** IV, Guarnaccia	$18.95
2096	**Silverplated Flatware**, Revised 4th Edition, Hagan	$14.95
1922	Standard **Old Bottle** Price Guide, Sellari	$14.95
3892	**Toy & Miniature Sewing Machines**, Thomas	$18.95
3828	Value Guide to **Advertising Memorabilia**, Summers	$18.95
3977	Value Guide to **Gas Station** Memorabilia	$24.95
3444	**Wanted to Buy**, 5th Edition	$9.95

ER

Schroeder's
ANTIQUES
Price Guide

. . . is the #1 best-selling antiques &
collectibles value guide on the market
today, and here's why . . .

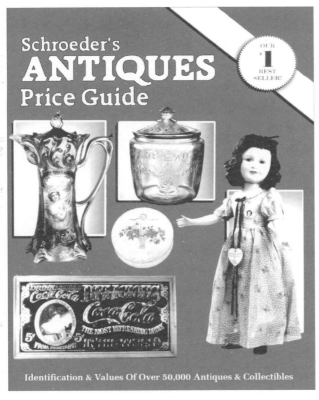

Schroeder's
ANTIQUES
Price Guide

OUR #1 BEST SELLER!

Identification & Values Of Over 50,000 Antiques & Collectibles

8½ x 11, 608 Pages, $14.95

• *More than 300 advisors, well-known dealers, and top-notch collectors work together with our editors to bring you accurate information regarding pricing and identification.*

• *More than 45,000 items in almost 500 categories are listed along with hundreds of sharp original photos that illustrate not only the rare and unusual, but the common, popular collectibles as well.*

• *Each large close-up shot shows important details clearly. Every subject is represented with histories and background information, a feature not found in any of our competitors' publications.*

• *Our editors keep abreast of newly developing trends, often adding several new categories a year as the need arises.*

If it merits the interest of today's collector, you'll find it in *Schroeder's*. And you can feel confident that the information we publish is up to date and accurate. Our advisors thoroughly check each category to spot inconsistencies, listings that may not be entirely reflective of market dealings, and lines too vague to be of merit. Only the best of the lot remains for publication.

Without doubt, you'll find
SCHROEDER'S ANTIQUES PRICE GUIDE
the only one to buy for
reliable information and values.

COLLECTOR BOOKS
A Division of Schroeder Publishing Co., Inc.